The Mending Worm

Joan Houlihan

New Issues Poetry & Prose

A Green Rose Book

New Issues Poetry & Prose
The College of Arts and Sciences
Western Michigan University
Kalamazoo, Michigan 49008

First Edition, 2006.

ISBN-10   1-930974-59-0 (paperbound)
ISBN-13   978-1-930974-59-3 (paperbound)

Library of Congress Cataloging-in-Publication Data:
Houlihan, Joan
The Mending Worm/Joan Houlihan
Library of Congress Control Number: 2005936537

Editor   Herbert Scott
Copy Editor   Curtis VanDonkelaar
Managing Editor   Marianne Swierenga

Art Director   Tricia Hennessy
Designer   Jean Bartha
Production Manager   Paul Sizer
                           The Design Center
                           School of Art
                           College of Fine Arts
                           Western Michigan University

The Mending Worm

Joan Houlihan

Joan Houlihan

For Alice,
Best wishes at
Brookline Booksmith
Nov 21, 2007

New Issues

WESTERN MICHIGAN UNIVERSITY

Also by Joan Houlihan

Hand-Held Executions, Poems & Essays

dedicated to my husband, Eric

Contents

I.

Squall Line	7
Ferrets	8
Unrelenting	9
Starke, North of Gainsboro	10
Orchard	11
In Cancer	12
Nothing So Stoic As a Child Done Early	13
Somnambulist	14
Ardor	15
The Infant Spouse	16
You Took from Me All Manner of Things	17
You Would Be Warm	18
Preparing Migration	19
Conversion	20
History Lessons	21
Hinge	22

II.

Why We Need Masks	27
One Cup	28
Ethan	29
The Last Inhabitant	30
Ilk	31
Maternal	32
And Everywhere Offering Human Sound	33
Mock Owls	34
Manikin	35
Preservation	36
The Tenders	37
Rationing, 1945	38
Enter the Time of Toil	39
Recovering Mother	40
Wife	41
Turn of a Year	42

III.

Nothing Else but You	47
Stuffed with Dark Cotton	48
Entering the Fourth Head	49

I Hear the Flood of Sunday Afternoons   50
You, Minus Delirium   51
Dahmers   52
Nux Vomica   53
Self-Scornings   54

IV.

Matter   59
From the Empire of Missing Uncles   60
Our New and Smaller Lives   61
The Way I Give It to You   62
As If Arising from a Rough Bed   63
Entitlement   64
Easter   65
Attending Brother   66
Wanting the Spider   67
All the Cold Mechanicals   68

V.

Hydrangeas   73
The Exhalation of Matty   74
Trouble Waking   75
Injury   76
Incarnate   77
Held   78
The Mending Worm   79

I.

Squall Line

In a farther sky rain gathers.
The smell is nickel. I long to replenish,

lean out like a dog, mouth sprung, tongue
loose, lapping the mineral air

because I must. In the quick theater of highway,
a low bird sidles to his bleed of meat.

C'est dommage. I've never been bitten—
only struck solemn, as in a parlor

where the hands lie crossed. Clouds bloat
the horizon. *Let's go back,* I say,

to the other version of us.
But we are taken with the scramble of rain

over weed, over bed-rolled hay—
the decant of all missed things.

Ferrets

From where they flourish in the night before
unable to stay unbred, they turn up dwarf

and dusky, primary as current and coil
in nested suburban explosion. Under stairs

by idiot light. At the tip of an abscess where god forms.
How you conduct your habit is up to you.

I have dragged you to where I can't care.
Memory, muscle, browse of fur

and sidelong, sizing eye—
a single animal, over again, residual in snow.

Unrelenting

If by succeeding you mean doing things right,
and exactly, then it has no future.
Ash blows from us madly and without cause.
To keep things the same, where do you stop
to worship and repair? It is natural to decline. I decline.

The modicum of life that strung the little necks
of crocuses, that lulled the feeble seed
into its disease called grass, that heaped the pious
branches with their only whiteness,
that broke silver from the jawbone of moon,

now walks me through the same lesson
of snow, until I am humble, until I am grateful,
until birches lean just far enough to undermine their spot.
As grass turns the color of last things, wheat and rope,
what can I do but walk over it.

Starke, North of Gainsboro

He is measured and fed and walked.
He is placed in the final chair.
He is swabbed and heat applied
along his skin. Each carpal of his wrist
quickly cracks to tinder sticks.

All that we can do is done:
the strapping and jolting, ceremonial
drubbing, the mummery and finger-play
behind his volted head. We hose him
as we would a tree, wrinkled and run deep

with char. The body, pinned and porous, shivers,
briefly sways, as if a damaged wall is lightly touched.
Empty-handed and incarnate, he is taken like a pet
and carried with his head cupped from behind.
Look on him. He is always ours, and cold.

Orchard

Elbow and arm held back,
Bent under every sky.
And I, not bridal

But dressed in a way
The world calls mean—
My cowl, my small-chewed sleeves—

Stand in a rigor of ice and mud.
My works and merits freeze.
Frost afflicts my eyes,

My skin is nickel and zinc,
And my astringent and desolate mouth—
All want the startle of flower, want

A pinhole of light,
And from these blonded, godly
Trees, favor, a spill of remedy.

In Cancer

Strung days, a puncture
and the insect entered.
You told me: *All dies.*
For this, we're intended.

Stung then by peonies'
heft and lush waste
bent-headed
I hid from the day.

Inside, the walls speckle.
Stark, kitchen-lit
flies pock the table
black as dropped seeds.

Though we go slowly
they startle—
bodies alive
with unshuttable eyes.

A simple swat exhausts us.
Let us forget. Let them flee
death. Their hum is harmless.

Our summer's begun
as the iris rises from sword-
shaped leaves, its veiny sac
a purse of grief.

Nothing So Stoic As a Child Done Early

Nettled over and backed against a marsh
of kept pools, in a filigree of gnats,

you can see it from the train—
whitened by evening and one light inside—

house to which you will come back.
You stood it for years.

In the cripple-fingered light, a few bees
squeezed through the screen

as you wound around each hand an urgent
maternal bandage. Accident?

You're stuttering. *Please*
open your throat for milk.

Somnambulist

I arose from bed as if incompletely burned.
Only unsteady, not a golem.
Not much of a talker, either.
Just mumbled through a cloth.

It must have been bred in the blood,
this hypnogogy. As much family
as my pouch of paltry things, my scruples.
Coming early from a last compassion

as soon as I had a mind to make
I'd go stand on high places: the altar's ledge,
the head of a saint. Not safe, a fanatic
without faith, a voice going through me:

Give me your winged and injured;
all the expiring breeds. I was so charmed
by the damaged. So difficult to reach.
Whatever it was that struck me came from beneath.

Ardor

I arrive to you as rain does:
sudden as a robe flung
open and urgent.

Let down the scarf
along your hair.

At the window, horses stand in a circle
calmed by hay, coat-damp,
steaming as from a snuffed blaze.

Turned out and without
such fortitude we will diminish—
unfairness of limbs, shrunken

valves unable to pump,
wind-crossed and in postures
modest and stooped.

There is only one way to speak of this:
as a joy no longer curable.

The Infant Spouse

Built and placed you in my body:
doll-sized, with a lung.
Gave you ear for listening long,
gave you mouth for suckling.
Made fists of cloth
and lickings for you, wax
for where the milktooth bites.
Scoured the wood around the crib,
made sacred for the kneeling.

When the surge and bulge began,
I raised you up and circled you
with ropy cord, to isolate. Came with bowls
of flaring oils—first to light, then feed you.
Always starving for me, staring,
numinous, attaching, never without tremble
or wet breath. A crippled light, half-

visible, I see you crossing Memorial Drive,
steady as an alcoholic, call to you,
take you home and tend your cratered heat.
What will I do without you, when alone?

You Took from Me All Manner of Things

In a room carved apart,
pinching the end of a hair
from this world, I am not let in
to the next. My fingertips stick
as to volted wire, teeth and bones
banging, cell-wracked. I am a wreckage

of light. Spring, its flood and buzz—
all counterfeit. Sweat bothers the back of my neck.
Will you rid me, make the wolf mild,
the hare, in its panic, soothe?
Not intact, not me, not ever, exactly, again
though I will be rid of season and cycle, be various

and multiple as grass, will go
where you would not have me.
Solitary as the mason bee
that leaves its nest to crumble,
I am intent to follow you, body left, hard.
Fast as you go, I will too—
cold, rabbit, and daft as moon.

You Would Be Warm

Just behind the altar, a clamor, and I am
displaced. Not rinsed or disinfected,
as even a knob of weed would be.

Who comes quietly, for you are far
and these swarm near.
It is not you I touch. You would be warm—
not small, and many, and cold.

Between you and me there is nothing
but body. Take it. I, weightless
over the gashed and corrugated
landscape, will no longer be stung

by the red, clear look of a poppy
nattered with black seed, no longer seen
by the one-eyed narcissus, nodding.

Dissilient as milkweed, deprived of cohesion,
I am a blown surface.

Preparing Migration

Perfected in high chambers, massed
among leaves, they are many-bodied
and ready to obey
as air changes to its one right pitch.

Inched into moth-hammered sleeves,
autumn feeds its hundred
as they mince along the branch
unstable in their need to lift, then

all wing and hinge, they rise.
This is the way I want you—
as long-awaited, as sudden.

Conversion

Eye to stranger eye, no place
for my mouth except on yours,
no place for my tongue
except to yours; salted
with owning, kneeling like a tree,
unreached by what I knew as sun,
I belonged to none but you.

Now as our conversation doubles back
the way a snow redoes its powder
on a lawn or eager spiders sift again
a single thread of web,
what was mortal empties out eternal;
what was covert and alone converts to us.

History Lessons

Lil' Ice Age

Ever felt baby knives whittle your face?
Penguins ramble 'round the bergs
not knowing better.
The sea has a mouthful of slush.
Get into your hole and pull up the cover.
Ice pricks. You should've eaten more blubber.

Age of Dirt

Worming into it and they don't have faces.
Wriggling makes it friable.
Everything's down there: rootball
like a giant's head stuck in,
mechanical ants finding purpose.
Small efforts add up.

Oracle Age

Some Athenian potter made the cup.
The fumes from it,
an expensive perfume.
Set on a tripod above a cleft,
sprig in her hand,
she huffed and uttered.
God though he was, Apollo
spoke through a woman.

Medieval Warming Period

Festooned, and some leg breeches
made of thick velvet. Hung with gold
so they could hardly walk. Pound for pound
their cups of silver shone best.
Marooned and meticulous monks sweated,
ruined their manuscripts.

Hinge

Born to this blocked light, aerial web
and rub of sun, one chafe of limbs
and the mating's done. Evening is an injury
of stars and on the trees a print
of something fungal, moving slow.

Let's take what's cut and left beneath the porch
for cold. Copper leaves leak red and bright.
What was once between us, damp and animal,
is spent. Forget how leaves are loosed
along the street but hear them go.

Pull on your gloves, the chambered wool.
We'll go to where the foolish door is batted
by the wind. Here's your hinge:
a rusted matter with a snapped pin.

$$\frac{22}{23}$$

II.

Why We Need Masks

To be god-ridden and demon-worthy, driven
to stagger, dance-drag under moon's bad
eye, rolled in motions of passing shades;

to revel in hungry otherness, tappings and hoots,
to back out of doors and run spinning; to set false fire,
laugh on birded lawns where all rise up, strung

invisible, little hung breaths. This too:
to be homely and hand-made, frost-spangled
and dotted with crimson, an hourglass spider

wobbly with poison, ready to dart.
For telling.
For incandescence.
For an honest noise in the dark.

One Cup

Stubborn, blunt-faced, you wander
the boat, doll's hair cropped
above the ears, nearly loved off.
The wake carves overtures

in the shape of a curling leaf.
You can't rest where all is bobbing
and wet, where the chance of octopus,
luxuries of squid, fill your eye.

Deeper down, sea cows browse. Union,
the point of liquid is union,
but you can't be fond, can you?
Only one cup left to drink from. Take it.

Narwhal rise rubbery over the place
they've encircled a calf,
their gust landing briefly on us.
The boat rocks, creaking like a crib.

Ethan

He cannot slake his need for us
and so keeps us away,
shakes off desire for company
as stamping boots would, the cling of clay.
In his own way he is warm, just unable. A hermit,
his only lesson, harm. I've seen him apart, hands over
a low-built fire. Refused, refusing, a recluse.
But whenever reckless, he will tilt,
tower-like, his pinnacle shadow, showing it
to himself there, on his own ground.

The Last Inhabitant

The acid cry, more than request—
it was etched black and stayed open.
You stopped in the mottled road to wait,
your face a knot of threat.

Summer spent its fever on lime and water,
bled the pent imagination.
The house filled with stalled air
and the last inhabitant walked away.

Here is the mind I made for you:
village hollow of people and ruled
by the weeper, light long out of him, time
a powder drifting from the mill.

How sage we've become, how dour,
nodding when we wish to speak—
and the moth-talk, the fuss of sheets and shades,
the reached hand drawn back,
the pause in its taking.

Ilk

An early form of menace made you
full of tooth and argument, my own.

Smaller in flight, you tuck under my arm
as we round shy towns, causeways,

powdered lawns. A mindless vicinity
now that we've lost body and beauty

now that we live through what we lived for—
the disquiet of love, slight proofs

it would make of presence and care.
My likeness, giddy, dying of memory

rosier toward death, soundproof
in the mouth, you came to me already harmed.

Maternal

Where on the shore did you say: *Meet me.*
Only mothers walk here, quit of the children.
Heel prints perforate a path.
The dogs lean, panting, into the spray.

After such a bout of child, the note
I must hold is longer, more broken than before.
Trees jut from scrub, as last things do
after a burning, the refuse still resting in the Y

of their limbs. Without instructions
for desertion, I've been clung to, marked
by eager hands. Don't look for me
in another place. There is no other place.

And Everywhere Offering Human Sound

Come here. Let me finger your hair.
The way you imitate weather:
the rush and sting of pinkened air
crows talking briefly of home
and then the pelted tree.
By these shall I know ye
bless yer little round mug.

My semiprecious, so much slow time
crawling and browsing
so much fascination with harmful insects
and corrosive sublimate.
As if you have as many eyes
as many eyes as the common fly,
and every one open wide
to the made world.

So, I get up at four a.m., finally, to put on some tea—
a soothing explanation for steam.
Children grow into themselves, then away.
We musn't worry when they're gone—
or not-quite-gone-yet.
The roots of things connect
where we can't see.

When I was born, my mother began counting
to herself. Something in the middle went missing.
But I have all my faculties.
In fact, I still remember to turn
every small thing until it gleams:
your favorite airplane pin

there, gliding on its cotton wad.
Now come here so I can see
in your eyes the sky within.
You are my only animal—
my animal of air.

Mock Owls

One is gone who trailed daylight, was favored
by fields, took the hot breath and gab
of August, morning and its mock owls.
Time steepens.

As to the origin, and pith, of loss:
I have no talk, just brace for the vertebra
askew, tapped clavicle, hip, pinned.
Whatever helps.

Made of distances now, I want less
and move with the stagger of something
dying down the day's green halls.
Wanting what's left.

Manikin

Lie down. I am hand and finger
to you, intent in my medium,
fluent in what flourished before
and guided by the noise of trapped being.

I was yours at birth, privy to your washings
and waste. Words spoken by us
are lysis and ligature. What matters
is the gash, the possible rush.

How to conduct the bleeding?
Bent to you, I provide from my fingers
something small and mammal,
harvested from one discarded.

Ten hours of us and we are wed.
Mumbling of vein, I finish you,
who will emerge new-made, doll-sewn,
the furthest thing from my mind.

Preservation

What the snow tells with its first and dirty melt
is leftover gristle, scat. Winter sticks
show through, skinned, almost metal
with an ice we remember. Night torsion

and a slick force harden our prints
prematurely. The surprise of breaking through,
the crackle—the sound of damage
stays on like a fact.

Some tinder struck in a spare room—
the spark, charge, and quick flare
cannot illuminate, snuffs, in one click of air
what cares for us. From corner to corner

the shouting ran—not to make us tell,
to make us unable to tell.
There are more dead than living down here—
iced, inside, where the shock is.

The Tenders

I see the women drifting
blued by certainties of ice
their crookedness tamed
into shapes of plain listening.
In cameos set against panoramas
they carry stick bundles—
arms skinned, faces damaged
by weather—the sweetness rubbed out.
Ice bristles our window. I tend you
as evening tends them—
bearing the small, cloth lamp.

Rationing, 1945

What stays massed in the mind
are instructions: render the fat,
reuse the tea; save, sure of the reason.

This was dread:
hardened, and solid as lard.
Grudges were holstered or held

to the light, their milkweed dispelled.
The sponge was wrung for its last.
We went together, washed and chagrined,

to wait for the cans, contents unknown.
Intent and covetous, lit by hunger,
we opened them, and complaints

disappeared in our mouths.
We went together at midday, at dusk,
to seize the fuel, the flour—

as some mother went weeping
against the wall—
to seize the milk, which was ours.

Enter the Time of Toil

Ants must carry the bodies of ants.
For this we are thankful, relieved—
after the drills, the shoving
shoes on, one after another
all the trample of happenstance—
to know we are born and bound to it.

But when snow takes over we stop,
uneasy at fields, garbled weeds,
postures of the harmless gone wrong.
Whatever laid down this cloak
of not knowing
makes standing mumblers of men

and the jitter of cop-light
rouses murder, its black startle-box
of stars. We hide this
the way snow hides the world—
with deliberate cold, built slow.

Recovering Mother

Marooned, autumnal, I think of your hands,
when women were linen and church,

when gloved and scented from a private drawer,
they folded, public and still.

How lawful, your scarf, but loose
at the neck. The expanse of your mouth

when it spoke: how lightly acidic
the cruelty held back. You met the condition

for being there: the half-seen grief
from a taking away, as scarring is left

when a branch is detached. Not wanting
a cinctured beauty, a history of *no*

sweetened by saints, the gravity of a bent body,
I was not right-minded and so would lie

with a feral stare, backtalking the divine.
To recover you now is wrong:

to force rearrangement of our tableau
into looking down, and away

from each other, postures animals take
to show they mean no harm.

Wife

She is bound to him,
Pressed against a hard place, then
Inside it, doorless. Do not prevent her.
She is bent to a matter made new, has gone
Intimate, abundant in it.
Compared with this
All else is riddle and fragile, cannot
Last, a stalk of freesia puffed tender,
Pulled down by its one-sided cluster.
For the head of a woman is god,
Each hair kept by a net of sun.

Turn of a Year

This is regret: or a ferret. Shuffling,
stunted, a snout full of snow.

As the end of day shuffles down
the repentant scurry and swarm—

an unstable contrition is born.
Bend down. Look into the lair.

Where newborn pieties spark and strike
I will make my peace as a low bulb

burnt into a dent of snow. A cloth to keep me
from seeping. Light crumpled over a hole.

Why does the maker keep me awake?
He must want my oddments, their glow.

$$\frac{42}{43}$$

III.

Nothing Else but You

With your trail of powder and devil shoes,
with a mill for hard and a bowl for spills
you're everybody's glamour rage
you're doom on a cracker with a dark red brew.

Crooked and flamed, broken-mother
chained, with bad and uncertified stare,
you were never chinked-up in a family fence
you were free—something wrong

and against. Now you're everybody's
take-me-home, black cuffs and fine
wreck of silks. You make us feel
we've been swapped down, needing

a borrow of light. You're everybody's
air and spark. Nothing but a lightning
bite. You've got wit, grit, and a tail to be lit—
the blade, the heel, and the screw.

Nothing else but you will do.
Not Little Sir Charm and his Finger Box.
Not Mistress Up-to-the-Sky.
Not Baby and her Blanky of Blue.

You got everything and more
and we want to be like you—
in this hatched-out drone of our insect hour,
in this cruel box of our days.

Stuffed with Dark Cotton

So I'm gluing distance together
with birdlime, grout and small wads
of wax, when in walks my attendant:
Time for your bath.
I am lowered into it, unfinished.

Once upon a time,
everybody could do everything.
Then it all got checked off:
best bully-pie. *Check.*
best ice-tickle. *Check.*
best finger-in-your-eye. *Check.*

Stuffed with dark cotton
I was put elsewhere.

Engine waste, the heat of youth,
keeps blowing in my face.
I'm dying to get through life
when in walks Aunty Grimell,
all pinking shears and failed teeth.

One look at her and my hair starts
grabbing out by the fistful. *Get out
and meet people,* she says.
So I join a freak stampede
hung all over with shredded
flags and gallop with the roans
and sorrows until the law cuffs me blind
and shows me the hole.

Now I'm sentenced to pry myself out
with the tines of a fork.
Don't worry. With careful digging,
I will unearth the perfect plank:
freckled and grained, with all the knots left in.

Entering the Fourth Head

Our good was declared and floated out to sea
in a tinder boat. Wind flicks the seagrass.

The sand is sinister with insects
and other small things that scuttle between us.

We're here for the monotony. To stop thought
at the borders, I roll up its flavor in a thin tissue

and place it across your mouth: Now breathe.
You will become brackened, corrupt. You will enter

the fourth head, the one they call wise.
Stepping deeper into voice and shirred places,

where the sea works sand into dents and warps,
we stand in tidal pools, with sticks. Each wave rears up,

a mesh of droplets: hush and back, swish and fall,
dragging a rattle of stones.

Along the brothy shore we ran,
large in the pelican's eye.

I Hear the Flood of Sunday Afternoons

Trees mingle. And your mouthprints—
all over the glass. So moody.
It's the weather. And this strap is too tight.

We find nasty chemicals in the cabinet,
corrosion of someone's will.
Junked sunlight all over the couch

and the minister's son, wearing the lining
of a coat, eyes shut against the rush,
disturbing inertia.

We remain eager for the animal
until the man comes—
all breath and teeth and enlarged garments.

I want to know nothing. I want to
consider the lady slipper—
how refined, how so like a delicate bladder.

Sit with me. Here,
hold this glass: water and blue
beauty, the dredged silt from a throat.

You, Minus Delirium

That you would have me, no substitute,
that I am your only intoxicant,
staggering gait and fever;
that I am your primary cranium
gauzy and not seen into,
makes me cry old.

I worship the house where we tried to live:
rooms afflicted with civet,
indwelling pocketed squirrels.
Even the light was ingenuous there,
the moon—makeshift, defective,
the sway of stars, massive.

This is how I reminisce: as if washing a wound
with citrus. Once hardy and nearly felon,
I meekly carve a spud
in the shape of a martyr's head.
Because you were greatly misunderstood
and I caused you such holy pain.

Dahmers

Present at the washing—
a condition, a child, a confinement.

Swing the light closer, hold it here.

Had sacrament and nothing moved.
Had memory ceremony.
Had hair grown blond, had close to the sun.

Seasons trying to see them, something always growing.
The white and wretched powder they called weather,
welcomed in, severe.

Pull on the glove and tweeze this bit.

Seclusion and the softest pump:
"Give us a grief, something to feel."
Snugged even closer, reduced together
they had a condition, a child.

The ligature was yellow. The stain's still on the skin.

Leaned toward it, swept it, dismissing the mess.
Calm but with an underfist.

And the body tore like that.
And the throat impaled.
Someone sawed and took the jaw,
unhinged it for a saving.

By a low cabinet, by instruments failing,
no comfort and none confided.
All the deceased have been buried, found.
They lift what remains, call it borne.

Nux Vomica

Your cough, your mental skeleton
don't scare me anymore. The head
you came with or your stiffened leg.
I got miles of teething rodent, open-eyed,
fully furred, crepitant along the cellar stair.

Brimful, I once flew at you no more
than codling moth and struggled in the fibrils
of your hair. Curious, you tweezed me
out and held me to the bulb,
your eye a tinted cellophane, and clear.

Now the murdered nests appear
and lurkers without wings, and crocus
sticks its little head, all purple, up for air.
The Nux Vomica flowers hard and toxically, my dear—
just like you and me this time of year.

Self-Scornings

Left to live downwind, uncombed,
clothed in rupture.
No comity but unripe fruit.
No relief but juice.

Why do they come?
They choke the goodness out,
disguise intent, keep tiny stabbers
inside their sleeves tipped against the wrist.

We will not recover from this.

What agitates, what is migrant in us?
It's why we keep my crying soft
until I knock back my supply
of soothe and sex, take another breath—
and begin to talk.

IV.

Matter

I make a little mother out of mud, sticks
and a bit of gauze. Once formed and dried,
she's bound to disappear: powder to my fingers.
All my plaster saints go down that way.
Wormwood. Gall. Rot.

Not that it matters, but
I once saw Mars through a telescope:
pockmarked, awash in gas, but distant enough
for dignity. All this farawayness has to stop.
So much homesickness, but so little home.

And so many notions they call *tradition.*
Knife, fork, whip of potatoes—all the womanly arts
are not so much lost as far, as spilled,
moved from the table too fast—
salt from a lidless box. And the one candle

I molded and set on the mantle had to be lit.
To enjoy the burning, Mother said.
Because something holy was happening then,
and all was made to be blown away—
expelled like a mouthful of air.

From the Empire of Missing Uncles

I want to tell something as simple as sky—
how you and I broke into long-legged crouches,
Groucho-ed across the backyard, how the moon
was shiny, a giant's hand-candy and how pumped
with laughter, that futile gas, we were helium-giddy
and the world was a fart-cushion spread
for a fat man's ass. I've said nothing to you
since you died, silt backed up to your throat.
But you know I've come back to you, small and denied,
for that penny arcade card you kept in your pocket—
tiny violin embossed in the corner—
until someone of ordinary sorrow was so deservingly solemn
you needed to mock them with a long-faced bow
and these words, formal and scrolled:

Please accept this card
as a token of my deepest sympathy.

Our New and Smaller Lives

Noonlit, mugged by heat, what we have
shrinks. Pores go small. We save, condense.

Standing the distance between us: blond fields,
a giddy weather of laughter and collapse

when hailstones popped on roofs, steam
haloed every grass. The pan we left grew tarry-black

and stuck. Now blight adheres, a frost,
as trees take down their light like medicine

straight to the rigor that ails them. Busy as mold
in our new and smaller lives, we do as we've been told

by those whose shoulders, late in windows, hunch,
whose hands we hear rummage. Be quiet

as must in a drawer. They still seek the perfect hour,
the one left elsewhere, struck.

The Way I Give It to You

Spotted with shade, daylilies lean
close at the roadside, deep in their fret
of weed. Let go, they will prosper.

Anything not stopped does that—takes
the air like a tonic. We are another occasion
of greed: smell, taste and such, then

in twenty-four years, fetal cells flush
from the mother's blood. As in purge.
As in waste. As in water from a ditch.

This news is so bad, I want it stark,
the way I give it to you: as a death
of something not loved,

to be let down slowly,
using our hands.
Something we can do together.

As If Arising from a Rough Bed

To put it behind me, the stain on flannel,
the rinsed smell of a house on Sunday—
I can't. I'm talking to it still:
how coming home, the sun converted
to a species of grass stamped with white,
how after church, the held let go,
how I chucked the high heels against
the wall and rolled on the warm rug
for pleasure.

What I tend these days is an infant
sly and watchful, as if every move is the one
I should have made. So I talk of Tucson,
of standing in gas station restrooms,
as if every move were a botch, as if
I haven't known the science of pure motion
that fans the blow, the heat of what I had to do.
How advanced I've become. How stricken
in years. How much the epicure of strife.
As if the shy standing before a man didn't count.

Entitlement

The natural arrival of parents:
tremulous, on stalks of age, they wave.
All the eaten years are downed.
They sit on beds, growing small.

It all fits into a box: interrogation, memory loss,
the sooted addiction to wish. I am packing sashes
and filaments, helmets of heavy cloth.
I am entitled to this.

Elected to fringe nobility,
blue races under their skin.
I accept their debris, deflected sparks,
the chewed-off ends of their speech.

Pulling a thumb, prying open a fist,
soothing them with their names, I walk them up
as they spike and fade. Mine is to pilot the fragile,
rocked slow in the motor of night.

Easter

We convene here, listen to Uncle B
in his backward-pointing baseball cap
lit with stories, muttering of loss—
a low and meaningless animal sound
we take for talk.

We have put it all behind us
and, spoon-fed with the whipped
milk of childhood, we revel in what's gone:
the rock of the undiscussed.

Mother's cataract and Father's altered
look give us nothing to say is wrong.
We lean into it, here
where the rock was struck
and the air inside stopped,

where unhinged stems root
and flower—
because that which was unknown
is not, and that which cannot
must rise and walk.

Attending Brother

We made humble music of father's shirts:
from laundered collars, slipped out tissue strips
blue and crisp, to lay along a comb
and hum against. How the pitch rose from lowdown
in the throat, travelled high, came out kazoo-y.
We fell against each other, happy.
And funnier, the headlines you would prop
at our formal table: *Man Drills Hole in His Own Head* or
Human Baby Born to Dog until mother grabbed at them
for trash and you in mock aggrievance bowed your head
and wouldn't eat. Such disturbances made us laugh.
But what was yours, that I can't raise an argument against
your being carried past, or the priest's two fingers pressed
against his lips through which he mumbles god.

Wanting the Spider

Born of some comet's heedless scatter
and disclosed on the hedge, you—

murderess of bees, one danger I needed
in a summer's rosary of enclosure: mothers

shouting me from their yards, the crossed knees
and sidelong eyes of my already knowing girlfriends,

the condescension of brothers, their freedom.
Barelegged in the nudge of grasshopper weed

I stood greedy, unable to pinch you, shy of the bite.
How it happens in the hierarchy of fields:

I show you to a friend who runs for a jar
to briskly cup you and screw down the lid.

He lets me visit, voyeur of my loss. My *tap-tap*
on your little prison. Your trembly, high-stilted walk.

All the Cold Mechanicals

As the hill assumed its dome of snow
and the least-frozen thing its life,
I assumed us. Singed with light
we sped downhill, stung fresh, tucked in.

I granted sky its steeling cloud, its lance
of branches, darker where we landed, snow
most chaste where legs and arms imprinted shapes,
left them diminishing continuously.

Our lightened sleds responded to our tugs
as night delayed by whitened hills—
all the cold mechanicals in place.
How much smaller we've grown, each season

rising unrefreshed, more empty of us.
Come to the window my childhood friend.
See the branches cast in snow again
and freckled over with melting.

$$\frac{68}{69}$$

V.

Hydrangeas

Salt air flutters them, cradles
their heads, lolling and solemn

as babies born slow. The heft
and bend is determined by stem,

by water, genetics, and sleight of wind.
We left what unsettles us to come here

where lengthy water unstops and spills,
mottled by sunset, crossed by gull,

immortality in a chamber of shell.
The children grow hairy and tall as they sleep.

Loose boats bruise the dock.
What the sea dredges up in the dark

this time, is sand tooth, fishbone, spine,
hard fruit of the tide, left where it's dropped.

Unnestled, we listen to salt air drift
across the hydrangeas; its sift.

The Exhalation of Matty

This is what stopped life looks like:
bulge-eyed, bog-mannish with an IQ of night.
We all felt for that. Then the charity ran out
for his habit, his way, and going

where others went, head in an angelbag,
fumed. Last known address was here,
where butane penetrated his clothes, where
he couldn't get held, where he went down

hard. When they hoisted him up,
the belt went slack. That was all to be done.
They locked him up in a man-sized box.
We all felt for that, and went home.

Trouble Waking

A peculiar tableau of debris—
masonry, furniture, still-living bodies—
has rushed from my grip, as water poured out.

Grave and with sacred utensils, workers
flashlight the spot. They are roaming
a comatose, toppled world

to locate the face of you.
There is no provision for me
save some strange eternities

arrayed for selection and kill.
As in: what is in store for your unborn,
high and dying in cells?

The close-held swarm of your afterthoughts,
a rarer, juvenile blue? Who did this to you
would also shed death on every way of mine.

Chosen persons, all those who grieve,
and all who knew me before,
can't deny I am changed.

The sediment from what's poured off
is somnolent, frontal, fragile.
What's left of you, white and discarnate.

Behind, the old life flows away.

Injury

What made you, little slam and fury,
feisty cupboard, shut?

How kept, how meager, still as cellar
but with will and want to do—

what place hives you, studs you with,
as if with stars, your stings?

Ashen, my sweet history, pointing
and the slack wrist after—

you are the same except the shirt
no longer kept of you.

When evening feelers make a wreck of sun,
how should I care?

I have my fraud,
that old and holy jewel of perfect days.

Be standing now and coated in the smash of that,
its tiny shinings, gracious as a rain.

You had a mind and it's a drift of fly.
I had a child—violent, unprepared—

who made of wisdom something small
and smothered in the grass.

What we never guessed, and harder heard
is what the dirt says, how it will go on, outlast.

Incarnate

Brought in by pulling you under the arms
as one would a carnal bulk or bagged weight.

In from an unsheltered water.
In from a lanterned shore, and left

the way a tide is, continuous and without intent.
A downing of air, then finger to lip pronounced you

gone. What's best kept close is this you, tiny—
your bed a fold, a night-shell. Your modest need

for rest and food. Your school of injury and song.
Now we can talk anywhere.

Held

On the gone water and on the going
death is a long story

as a cuttlefish produces ink
and from a tree is born its shadow

every day will be stilled by sorrow

slow and toward as oil
a narcissus of dying things

massed to a far bottom
an infusion of tar and mercury

faithful to its matter
where black flowers grow and velvet.

Come October, with your fogs on the river.

The Mending Worm

Through pores of earth
the mending worm threads, each green

a separate compulsion. In the house
where our fears are privately boxed, we wake.

Now is the time to remove the cloth
that warms and protects our throats.

Morning breathes steamy shapes on the car.
Magnolia skins litter the yard.

Easter comes early—
cups and cutouts, pinwheels and horns—

toy beauty so long in the ground.
This is what I want: to return

the same way I came. Now you join my impossible
travel, child at the start of a man,

your silhouette tensed in windshield light
and the new way you speak: lower, far down.

Acknowledgements

Grateful acknowledgment to the editors of the following publications in which these poems first appeared:

Bayou, Black Warrior Review, Born Magazine, Boston Review, Caffeine Destiny, Columbia: A Journal of Literature and Arts, CrossConnect, Del Sol Review, Fine Madness, Gettysburg Review, Gulf Coast, Harvard Review, Larcom Review, Marlboro Review, Passages North, Poetry International, Spoon River Poetry Review, VOLT

The Iowa Anthology of New American Poetries, edited by Reginald Shepherd; *March Hares: The Best Poems From Fine Madness*, edited by Sean Bentley, John Malek, Anne Pitkin, and Judith Skillman.

Immense gratitude to my husband, Eric Howlett, for his steadfast belief in me and for his always precise and honest comments, and to all those who encouraged and helped shape the poems: Pamela Alexander, Daniel Bosch, Adam Dressler, Donna Johnson, Vera Kroms, Michael Perrow, Lynne Potts, Beth Woodcome, Susan Zielinski and all the Sargent Street regulars. Thanks for supporting and believing in my work to: Fred Marchant, Ander Monson, Michael Neff, Reginald Shepherd, Dan Woods, and Franz Wright. Thank you also to the Concord Poetry Center, and especially to Lucie Brock-Broido for knowing the why and wherefore of these poems, and for her invaluable help with this manuscript.

photo by Eric Howlett

Joan Houlihan is author of *Hand-Held Executions, Poems &*
Essays (Del Sol Press, 2003). She is founding director of the
Concord Poetry Center in Concord, Massachusetts, where she
also teaches.

New Issues Poetry

Editor, Herbert Scott

Vito Aiuto, *Self-Portrait as Jerry Quarry*
James Armstrong, *Monument in a Summer Hat*
Claire Bateman, *Clumsy, Leap*
Kevin Boyle, *A Home for Wayward Girls*
Michael Burkard, *Pennsylvania Collection Agency*
Christopher Bursk, *Ovid at Fifteen*
Anthony Butts, *Fifth Season, Little Low Heaven*
Kevin Cantwell, *Something Black in the Green Part of Your Eye*
Gladys Cardiff, *A Bare Unpainted Table*
Kevin Clark, *In the Evening of No Warning*
Cynie Cory, *American Girl*
Peter Covino, *Cut Off the Ears of Winter*
Jim Daniels, *Night with Drive-By Shooting Stars*
Darren DeFrain, *The Salt Palace* (fiction)
Joseph Featherstone, *Brace's Cove*
Lisa Fishman, *The Deep Heart's Core Is a Suitcase*
Robert Grunst, *The Smallest Bird in North America*
Paul Guest, *The Resurrection of the Body and the Ruin of the World*
Robert Haight, *Emergences and Spinner Falls*
Mark Halperin, *Time as Distance*
Myronn Hardy, *Approaching the Center*
Brian Henry, *Graft*
Edward Haworth Hoeppner, *Rain Through High Windows*
Cynthia Hogue, *Flux*
Joan Houlihan, *The Mending Worm*
Christine Hume, *Alaskaphrenia*
Josie Kearns, *New Numbers*
David Keplinger, *The Clearing*
Maurice Kilwein Guevara, *Autobiography of So-and-So: Poems in Prose*
Ruth Ellen Kocher, *When the Moon Knows You're Wandering, One Girl Babylon*
Gerry LaFemina, *The Window Facing Winter*
Steve Langan, *Freezing*
Lance Larsen, *Erasable Walls*
David Dodd Lee, *Abrupt Rural, Downsides of Fish Culture*
M.L. Liebler, *The Moon a Box*
Deanne Lundin, *The Ginseng Hunter's Notebook*
Barbara Maloutas, *In a Combination of Practices*
Joy Manesiotis, *They Sing to Her Bones*
Sarah Mangold, *Household Mechanics*

Gail Martin, *The Hourglass*
David Marlatt, *A Hog Slaughtering Woman*
Louise Mathias, *Lark Apprentice*
Gretchen Mattox, *Buddha Box, Goodnight Architecture*
Paula McLain, *Less of Her, Stumble, Gorgeous*
Lydia Melvin, *South of Here*
Sarah Messer, *Bandit Letters*
Malena Mörling, *Ocean Avenue*
Julie Moulds, *The Woman with a Cubed Head*
Marsha de la O, *Black Hope*
C. Mikal Oness, *Water Becomes Bone*
Bradley Paul, *The Obvious*
Katie Peterson, *This One Tree*
Elizabeth Powell, *The Republic of Self*
Margaret Rabb, *Granite Dives*
Rebecca Reynolds, *Daughter of the Hangnail, The Bovine Two-Step*
Martha Rhodes, *Perfect Disappearance*
Beth Roberts, *Brief Moral History in Blue*
John Rybicki, *Traveling at High Speeds* (expanded second edition)
Mary Ann Samyn, *Inside the Yellow Dress, Purr*
Ever Saskya, *The Porch is a Journey Different From the House*
Mark Scott, *Tactile Values*
Hugh Seidman, *Somebody Stand Up and Sing*
Martha Serpas, *Côte Blanche*
Diane Seuss-Brakeman, *It Blows You Hollow*
Elaine Sexton, *Sleuth*
Marc Sheehan, *Greatest Hits*
Heidi Lynn Staples, *Guess Can Gallop*
Phillip Sterling, *Mutual Shores*
Angela Sorby, *Distance Learning*
Matthew Thorburn, *Subject to Change*
Russell Thorburn, *Approximate Desire*
Rodney Torreson, *A Breathable Light*
Robert VanderMolen, *Breath*
Martin Walls, *Small Human Detail in Care of National Trust*
Patricia Jabbeh Wesley, *Before the Palm Could Bloom: Poems of Africa*